# OLYMPIC GAMES

BY M.G. HIGGINS

# NONFICTION

Cryptocurrency

Deadly Bites

Digital Worlds

Droids and Robots

Esports

Flight Squads

**Olympic Games**

Working Dogs

World Cup Soccer

EDUCATIONAL PUBLISHING
www.sdlback.com

**Photo credits:** page 2: railway fx/Shutterstock.com; page 4/5: Ververidis Vasilis/Shutterstock.com; page 7: Creative Photo Corner/Shutterstock.com; page 10: maxim ibragimov/Shutterstock.com; page 16: Olga Popova/Shutterstock.com; page 24: marchello74/Shutterstock.com; page 27: Eric Broder Van Dyke/Shutterstock.com; page 32: INTERFOTO/Alamy Stock Photo; page 40: PA Images/Alamy Stock Photo; page 40: Mitch Gunn/Shutterstock.com; page 41: Leonard Zhukovsky/Shutterstock.com; page 43: dpa picture alliance/Alamy Stock Photo

ISBN-13: 978-1-68021-738-4
eBook: 978-1-63078-908-4

Printed in Malaysia

24 23 22 21 20    1 2 3 4 5

# Table of Contents

# A Global Event

An Italian **underdog** wins gold. A star player from Japan sets a record. Their stories inspire. The action pulls people in. Every two years, the Olympics **unite** the world.

The Olympic Games began thousands of years ago. They were first held in Greece. Early contests were popular but small. There was only one race, and just a few people took part. Much has changed since then.

Today, the Games are two huge events. One is held during the summer. The other is in the winter. There are many sports. Thousands of athletes come from around the world to compete. Each one wants to be the best. Who will take home a medal?

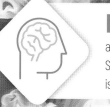

**FAST FACT:** The Olympic Games are made up of sports. Each sport has events. Swimming is a sport. The 200-meter backstroke is an event.

# Making It Happen

Cities are picked to host the Games. Hosts are responsible for everything the event needs. Hosting is a big honor. But it is not easy to pull off. There is much to do to prepare. Sports arenas must be built. Safety has to be planned for. Expenses can add up quickly. Some cities struggle to make it all happen.

There are benefits to hosting the event. Host cities are put in the public eye. People wonder how they will top the previous Games. Billions tune in to find out. Media rights bring in big money. Cash flows in from tourists too. It is not always enough to cover the cost of hosting. This is a risk some cities are willing to take.

**FAST FACT:** About 3.6 billion people watched the 2016 Summer Games on TV. Nearly half the world tuned in.

# THE OLYMPIC FLAG

There are five rings on the Olympic flag. They link together. This is meant to show unity. Each ring is colored for the flags of the countries that took part in the 1912 Games. The top rings are blue, black, and red. The bottom two are yellow and green. The Olympic flag was designed in 1912. It was first flown at the 1920 Games.

# The Will to Win

The Games can be hard on athletes. They want to do their best and make their country proud. Players are under a lot of pressure. Their training is intense. Few will even make it to the Games. Most who do will not win a medal. But it is the chance of a lifetime. For many, the sacrifices are worth it.

# What Is Next?

Scandal fills the world of sports. The Games are no exception. Officials have taken bribes from hosts. Drugs help athletes win. **Conflict** turns whole countries against each other. Still, the events continue.

What does the future look like for the Games? Many see the benefits of bringing the world together through sports. But there are complex issues surrounding the events. Changes are likely coming.

**FAST FACT:** The Winter and Summer Games used to be held in the same year. That changed after 1992. The Games were moved to two years apart. This gave winter sports more attention.

# The Early Games

Ancient Greeks liked sports. They enjoyed competition too. It is no surprise they created the Games. The event let them show off their strength and speed.

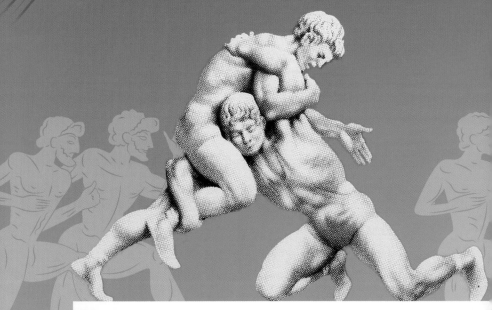

# Big Differences

The word *Olympics* comes from Olympia. This was a sacred site in Greece. The first Games were held there. It is hard to say when they began. Early writings suggest 776 BC. Experts think it was probably earlier.

These contests were not like those of today. They honored the Greek god Zeus. There were no teams. Each man competed for himself. People loved watching the event. Crowds were small though. Most who went lived nearby.

**FAST FACT:** There were four years between each Olympics. The ancient Greeks named this period of time. They called it an Olympiad.

# More Sports and Fans

At first there was only one event. It was a footrace called the *stade*. People ran for about 200 yards. Another race was added in 724 BC. This one was twice as long.

More sports were soon played. Wrestling started in 708 BC. The pentathlon began then too. This sport had five events. Men ran, jumped, and wrestled. They also threw a spear and a discus.

The Games lasted five days by 632 BC. The number of fans grew too. As many as 40,000 people watched. They came from across the Greek empire.

**FAST FACT:** The pentathlon is still an Olympic sport. But there have been changes. Today, there are swimming, fencing, and horse-riding events. Players must also run and shoot pistols.

# PANKRATION

Pankration means "all force" in Greek. The sport was very dangerous. Men used wrestling moves. Boxing blows were okay too. Players could not poke eyes or bite. There were few other rules. Even breaking bones was okay. Matches were not timed. Players had to give up. Some gave a signal they could not go on. Others passed out or even died. Greek fans loved this sport. Men needed more than just physical strength to win. They also needed to be smart and skilled.

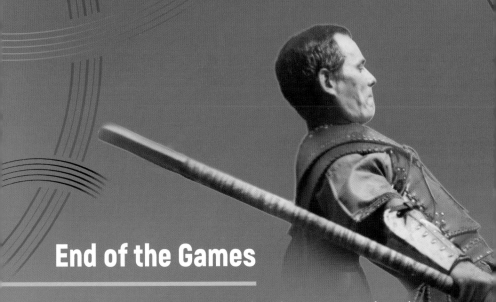

# End of the Games

Several hundred years went by. The event continued
to grow. Then there was a great war. Greece fell to
Rome in 146 BC. The Romans kept the Games going.
They liked sports too. But things began to change.
Athletes no longer played for honor. Winning became
about personal gain. Some players cheated. Winners
were worshipped like gods.

A new emperor rose to power. He believed in a single
god. Pagan worship of many gods had to stop. This
included events. One was the Games. They were last
played in the year 393. It would be a long time before
they came back.

**FAST FACT:** Married women could not watch or compete in the Games. But unmarried women could. There was even a separate event for them. It was a short footrace to honor the goddess Hera.

# A Revival

It was 1890. Nearly 1,500 years had passed. A French man traveled to England. His name was Pierre de Coubertin. While there, he met a man who loved sports. The man was trying to restart the Games. Coubertin was inspired. He wanted to help.

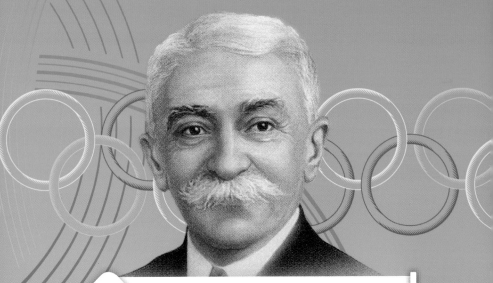

**FAST FACT:** The IOC still runs the Games today. It is based in Switzerland. There may be up to 115 members. They are from all over the world.

In 1894, Coubertin held a meeting. People came from nine countries. Everyone agreed the event should come back. This was an important meeting. It was the start of the IOC. That stands for International Olympic Committee.

The Games began again in 1896. Athens hosted. Over 240 men from 14 countries took part. They played nine sports. Some raced bikes. Others swam and wrestled. There were 43 events in all. More than 60,000 fans showed up. The revival was a big success.

## STRANGE SPORTS

New sports are added to the Olympics each year. Some are also taken away. Club swinging began with the 1904 Games. A man would twirl a club like a baton. He would earn points for his routine. Pigeon shooting was in the 1920 Games. The winner shot 21 live pigeons. About 300 birds were killed in all. People thought it was too bloody. The event lasted just one year. Today, people shoot clay discs instead. Tug-of-war was once an Olympic sport too.

# Women Join In

The next Games were in Paris. They were held in 1900. Close to 1,000 athletes took part. Among them were 22 women. These were the first women to compete in the Games. Before this, only men had been allowed.

Paris hosted again in 1924. More people wanted to compete. There were around 3,000 athletes total. They came from 44 countries. Over 100 of them were women.

# The Winter Games

The 1920 Games had two winter sports. One was figure skating. Ice hockey was the other. IOC members wanted to set these sports apart. They had an idea. There should be a separate event.

Winter Sports Week began in 1924. Athletes skied and skated. Some played ice hockey. There was bobsledding too. This was the first Winter Games. The name change became official in 1925.

**FAST FACT:** Women were not allowed to compete in all Olympic sports until 2012. Today, nearly half of all athletes in the Games are women.

## THREE MORE GAMES

There are other Games. One is the Special Olympics. They are for people with intellectual disabilities. These include autism and down syndrome. The first Special Olympics were held in 1968. Kids as young as eight can compete. The Paralympics were first held in 1960. Athletes who compete have physical disabilities. Some are deaf or blind. Others are missing limbs. Thousands of athletes attend. They come from over 160 countries. In 2010, the Youth Olympic Games began. They are called YOG for short. Teens ages 15 to 18 can compete. Thousands come from around the world.

# 4 Host Cities

Finding a host city used to be simple. There were fewer sports and fans. Almost any large city would work. Then the Games grew. Now it is harder to pick a host. Cities must bid to hold the event. The IOC picks the best offer.

**FAST FACT:** The 1976 Winter Games needed a host. Denver was picked in 1970. But voters did not want to pay. The city backed out in 1972.

# Choosing a Host

Not all cities can host. Certain requirements must first be met. Millions of people must be kept safe. They also need a place to stay. All sports must have arenas too. New structures may need to be built. Costs add up fast. The host must be able to pay. New taxes are often part of the plan. Taxpayers must agree.

Hosts are picked early. Decisions are made seven years in advance. First a city must apply. IOC members look closely at each bid. Some cities make the cut. Each must then pay a fee. Next, the IOC votes. It can take several rounds. The whole process takes two years.

# Bribes

Some cities break rules to become hosts. This happened in the U.S. Salt Lake City wanted to hold the 2002 Games. IOC members visited the location. There they were given expensive gifts. These were worth over a million dollars. It was a bribe.

In 1995, Salt Lake City won the bid. Then people found out about the gifts. It became big news. The IOC took action. Six members were kicked out. Others left on their own. There were rule changes too. Members would no longer visit bid cities.

**FAST FACT:** Athletes need a place to stay at the Games. Host cities build a special area. It is called the Olympic Village. Trainers stay here too.

## THE OLYMPIC IDEAL

The IOC has an ideal. It is peace and a better world. Host nations need to represent this. It has been an issue for some. One was China. It put in a bid for the 2000 Games. But the country did not promote human rights. It lost to Australia. China tried again for the 2008 Games. This time it won. The host city would be Beijing. Some countries were upset. They disagreed with the IOC's choice. Many said China had not done enough to improve human rights.

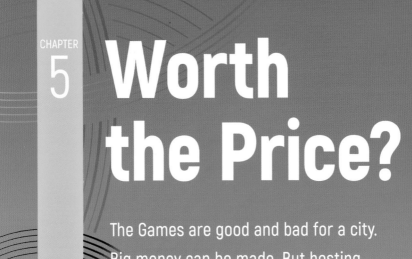

# Worth the Price?

The Games are good and bad for a city. Big money can be made. But hosting is expensive. Many hosts are left with serious **debt**.

# Big Money

A host city is in the spotlight. Its best features can be put on display. Everyone sees what it has to offer. Interest in the city grows. Some people will go for the Games. Others might travel there later. Tourism is good. It brings in big money.

Companies notice the city too. It could be good for business. Firms may open new offices there. This creates jobs and brings in more people.

The media covers the event closely. Host cities take a share of TV rights. Money comes from ad deals too. It is all worth billions.

**FAST FACT:** It cost more than $20 billion to host the 2016 Summer Games in Rio de Janeiro. The city covered over $13 billion of this on its own.

# Paying It Off

Making money from the Games is great. There is a problem though. Hosting often costs more than a city earns. This can put a city in big trouble.

Montreal held the Games in 1976. The city went $1.5 billion in debt. It took almost 30 years to pay it off. Athens held the 2004 Games. The debt was huge. Eventually Greece went bankrupt.

**FAST FACT:** Japan has asked people to turn in old cell phones. Parts inside are made of gold, silver, and bronze. The metal is being used to make medals for the Games.

# MAKING MONEY

Only one city has ever made a profit hosting the Olympics. It was Los Angeles. The 1984 Games were held there. Most cities build structures just for the Games. They hope to use them again later. But that often does not happen. Buildings sit empty. Los Angeles already had structures in place. This helped the city save money.

The 1984 Games were not sponsored by the government. This was a first. Funding came from companies. Private donors also helped. TV deals did too. Los Angeles made $215 million after all costs were paid.

# The True Cost of Hosting

ORIGINAL BUDGET | FINAL COST

IN BILLIONS (U.S. dollars)

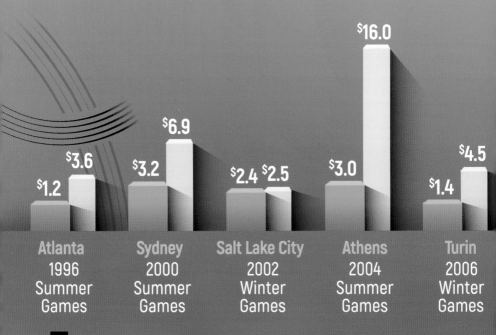

| | Atlanta 1996 Summer Games | Sydney 2000 Summer Games | Salt Lake City 2002 Winter Games | Athens 2004 Summer Games | Turin 2006 Winter Games |
|---|---|---|---|---|---|
| Original Budget | $1.2 | $3.2 | $2.4 | $3.0 | $1.4 |
| Final Cost | $3.6 | $6.9 | $2.5 | $16.0 | $4.5 |

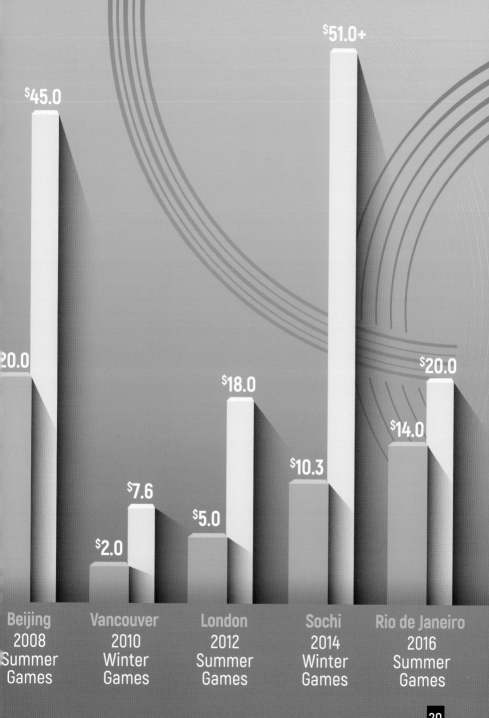

$45.0

$51.0+

20.0

$18.0

$20.0

$7.6

$10.3

$14.0

$2.0

$5.0

Beijing
2008
Summer
Games

Vancouver
2010
Winter
Games

London
2012
Summer
Games

Sochi
2014
Winter
Games

Rio de Janeiro
2016
Summer
Games

29

# Safety First

Safety at the Games is a top priority. The event is often a target for crime. Security is expensive. But the money must be spent. The 1972 Games show why. Munich hosted that year. This is a city in Germany. Terrorists had planned an attack. They took 11 athletes hostage. All were killed.

Today, officials try to stop crime before it starts. Good security is key. Rio held the Games in 2016. The city had a security force of 85,000. Most were police officers. Around 23,000 were soldiers. There were also over 1,000 spies. They were sent from the U.S.

# Cyberattacks

South Korea held the 2018 Winter Games. The nation was in conflict with North Korea. Some people thought the North might launch a missile. That did not happen. But cyberattacks did.

Devices stopped working. People at the stadium could not get online. The Games website went down. TV access was blocked too. Hackers may have tried to steal data. It is unclear who was behind the attack. Whoever it was, they successfully interrupted the event.

**FAST FACT:** Rio had another kind of safety issue. It was the deadly Zika virus. Some athletes were afraid. They did not want to catch it. Several decided to stay home.

# CHAPTER 6

# Troubled Past

Countries do not always get along. They show their anger in many ways. Sometimes it is through the Games. One way is with **boycotts**. This is when people refuse to take part in something.

## JESSE OWENS

The U.S. sent 18 African Americans to the 1936 Games. They won 8 gold medals. Jesse Owens was a star runner. He won four gold medals and set three world records. Owens was a hero. But he faced bias as a black man. He had to travel third class by ship to Berlin. The U.S. president did not shake his hand when he got home.

# Unfair Games

IOC members voted in 1931. Berlin would host the 1936 Games. This is a city in Germany. There, Adolf Hitler led the Nazi Party. It rose to power in 1933. The Nazis had rules for the event. One said no blacks or Jewish people.

Many countries were upset by this. There was even talk of a boycott. But it did not happen. The event went on. Nearly 50 countries took part. They sent almost 4,000 athletes. Several were black. A few were Jewish. Some athletes chose not to go.

# Taking Sides

Moscow held the 1980 Games. They did not go as planned. In 1979, the Soviet Union sent troops to Afghanistan. The U.S. president said to remove them. He would not send a team if they stayed. The Soviets said no. Many nations sided with the U.S. A total of 65 countries did not send teams.

The next Games were in 1984. They were held in Los Angeles. The Soviet Union got back at the U.S. by not sending a team. Its athletes were the best at the time. Soviet allies did not send teams either. This led to a one-sided event. Team U.S.A. won 174 medals.

# Last-Minute Teams

When South Korea hosted in 2018, there was conflict. Many worried about safety and security. Still, North Korea was allowed to attend. This upset the U.S. The two countries were at odds. The U.S. threatened to boycott the Games. But in the end, it sent a team.

**FAST FACT:** The Soviet Union fell in 1991. This marked the end of the cold war. All countries attended the 1992 Games. There were no boycotts. It was the first time in 20 years.

# Making It to the Games

Joining an Olympic team is a dream for many athletes. It is not easy to do. Training is tough. The hours are long. Only the best make the cut.

## Training

Athletes train hard for the Games. Many practice several hours each day. Some start very young. Their age depends on the sport. Gymnasts might begin at three. Bobsledders may be 25. Younger athletes must still go to school. Training happens during their free time.

Getting hurt can end a career. Staying fit is key. Players eat healthy foods. They also drink a lot of water. Exercise is important. Rest is too. This helps the body recover.

# Getting Picked

Special groups are in charge of each sport. They watch top athletes perform. Some groups hold trials. Athletes compete against each other. Others judge how players do over time.

Each group picks the best athletes. They make a list for their NOC. This stands for National Olympic Committee. Every country has one. Then the NOCs narrow each list. The IOC makes the final call. It decides who goes to the Games.

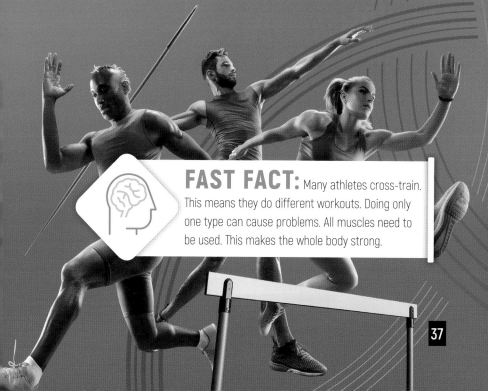

**FAST FACT:** Many athletes cross-train. This means they do different workouts. Doing only one type can cause problems. All muscles need to be used. This makes the whole body strong.

# Money Matters

Athletes need to earn a living. But there is little time to work while training. Some players find part-time jobs. Others have **sponsors**. Big stars can make millions.

The NOC in America is the U.S. Olympic Committee (USOC). This is a private group. It does not get money from the government. Instead, people can donate. Companies can too. Some of this money goes to athletes. They use it to pay for training. Their healthcare and housing costs are also covered.

**FAST FACT:** Sponsors are companies that give athletes money. In turn, players represent them. A sponsored athlete might wear clothing with the company's logo.

# The Price of Gold in 2018

The USOC also gives money to medal winners.
Earnings are split between players on a team.

GOLD MEDALISTS EARNED
**$37,500**

SILVER MEDALISTS EARNED
**$22,500**

BRONZE MEDALISTS EARNED
**$15,000**

# Best of the Best

The Games are all about sport. Athletes are the best in their event. Some break world records. They become stars. Many are Americans.

**FAST FACT:** The heptathlon has seven events. Athletes run two sprints and jump hurdles. They high jump and long jump. They also throw the shot put and javelin.

# On the Track

Jackie Joyner-Kersee went to four Games. Her first was in 1984. The track star won many medals. Three of these were golds. One was silver. She also won two bronze. In 1998, she set a world record. It was in the heptathlon. Her record has stood for over 20 years.

# In the Pool

Some say Michael Phelps is the best athlete ever. The swimmer won six golds in 2004. In 2008, he took home eight more. Phelps earned 28 medals total over five Games. This included 23 golds. He **retired** after the 2016 Games.

Katy Ledecky is another swimmer. She won her first gold at age 15. Her time broke a record. This was at the 2012 Games. Ledecky set two more records in Rio in 2016. Five of her six medals are golds.

# Winter Stars

Apolo Anton Ohno is a speed skater. He went to the Games three times. His speed earned him eight medals. Two of them were golds.

Tara Lipinski won a gold medal in 1998. She was only 15. This makes her the youngest figure skater to ever win gold.

Many think snowboarding stars are fun to watch. Shaun White is one of them. He won three golds in as many Games. The halfpipe is his big event.

**FAST FACT:** Michael Phelps has won more medals than any athlete in the Games. He has also broken 39 world records.

# WORST OF THE BEST

Some athletes will do anything to win. They may even turn to violence. Nancy Kerrigan was a figure skater. She was training hard. Her goal was to make the U.S. Olympic team. One day after practice, she was attacked. Someone hit the back of her leg with a club. It was one month before the 1994 Games. The facts came out later. A rival skater had played a role. Her name was Tonya Harding. Harding's ex-husband planned the attack. He hired a hit man. Both women went to the Games. Kerrigan won silver. Harding finished eighth. She was later banned from figure skating in the U.S.

# The Need to Win

Athletes want to win. Their goal is to bring home gold. They push themselves hard. It may not be enough. Some turn to drugs for a boost. This could help a player win. But is it worth the risk?

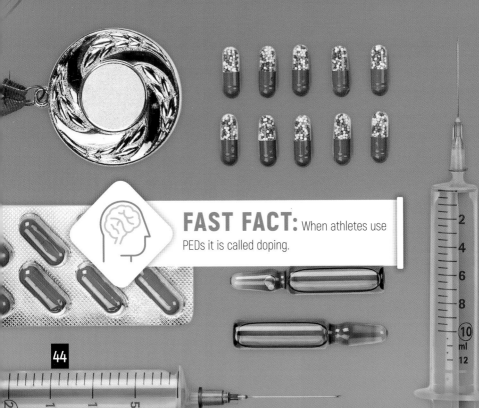

**FAST FACT:** When athletes use PEDs it is called doping.

# Drugs

The Games have a history of drug use. Early Greeks used herbs. They ate animal hearts too. These were thought to make people stronger.

Today some players take steroids. These help them build muscle. Other drugs are also used. They are called PEDs. That is short for performance-enhancing drugs. Physical activity is tiring. Players may want to stop. PEDs can keep them going.

## PEDS

Athletes use many kinds of performance-enhancing drugs. Steroids strengthen muscles. Hormones bulk up muscles too. Some PEDs help get more oxygen into the blood. This keeps athletes going longer without getting tired. Stimulants give energy. There are many other PEDs. Almost all pose risks. They can hurt long-term health. They can even kill. Plus an athlete will never know: Did they win because they were the best? Or was it the drugs?

Most drugs are banned from the Games. The IOC tests athletes before the event. It tests them after too. Sometimes PED use is easy to spot. This is not always the case. Certain drugs hide others. Some players do not get caught. Many do.

## When Winners Lose

Ben Johnson is a Canadian sprinter. He set a world record in the 100-meter dash. This was at the 1988 Games. Johnson took a drug test a few days later. The results were clear. PEDs had helped him win. The IOC removed Johnson's record. It took away his medal too. Carl Lewis had placed second in the race. Now the gold went to him.

Marion Jones is an American. Her event is track and field. At the 2000 Games, she won five medals. Jones denied using PEDs. Later she was caught in her lie. She spent six months in jail. The IOC erased her name from the record books. It took back her medals too.

**FAST FACT:** The IOC has been testing for PEDs since 1968. A special program was started in 1999. It is called the World Anti-Doping Agency, or WADA.

# Trouble in Russia

Russia held the 2014 Winter Games. Russian athletes did very well. Many also failed drug tests after the event. The IOC looked into this.

The players were at fault. Russian sports officials were too. They gave the players PEDs. Over 1,000 athletes had taken them. Some were banned from future Games. Several lost their medals. The country also had to pay a fine. It was $15 million.

Russian athletes were tested again. This was before the 2016 Games. The IOC cleared 271 players to compete. It banned 118.

Then the 2018 Winter Games were held. Some Russian athletes could go. But there was a catch. They could not play for their country. Their team was called OAR. This meant Olympic Athletes from Russia. Two players still failed drug tests.

**FAST FACT:** The entire Russian track-and-field team was banned from the 2016 Summer Games.

# CHAPTER 10

# Future Games

The Games face several problems. Cities do not want to lose money. Not all athletes play fair. Safety concerns are also growing. Weather is causing trouble too. Many people are looking for solutions. They want to see the event continue.

**FAST FACT:** Experts have many ideas about how to fight climate change. One is for countries to release fewer greenhouse gases. This could help, but it might not be enough.

# No Snow, No Games

Snow is needed for winter sports. But Earth is slowly warming. Experts call this climate change. Some cities get less snow now than in the past. It is only getting worse. Soon they may not be able to hold future Games.

One fix is fake snow. It is made by machines. This is expensive. Large amounts are not easy to make. Fake snow is also lower quality. Natural snow is better.

# Losing Locations

By 2022, 21 cities will have hosted the Winter Olympics. But these cities may not be able to host future Games if global warming continues unchecked.

| HOST CITY | HOST YEAR(S) | CLIMATE I |
|---|---|---|
| Chamonix | 1924 | ❄ |
| St. Moritz | 1928, 1948 | ❄ |
| Lake Placid | 1932, 1980 | ❄ |
| Garmisch-Partenkirchen | 1936 | ❄ |
| Oslo | 1952 | ❄ |
| Cortina d'Ampezzo | 1956 | ❄ |
| Squaw Valley | 1960 | ❄ |
| Innsbruck | 1964, 1976 | ❄ |
| Grenoble | 1968 | ❄ |
| Sapporo | 1972 | ❄ |
| Sarajevo | 1984 | ❄ |
| Calgary | 1988 | ❄ |
| Abertville | 1992 | ❄ |
| Lillehammer | 1994 | ❄ |
| Nagano | 1998 | ❄ |
| Salt Lake City | 2002 | ❄ |
| Turin | 2006 | ❄ |
| Vancouver | 2010 | ❄ |
| Sochi | 2014 | ❄ |
| Pyeongchang | 2018 | ❄ |
| Beijing | 2022 | ❄ |

 Cold Enough to Host

 May Be Too Warm to Host

🔥 Too Warm to Host

| ...0 | CLIMATE IN 2050 | CLIMATE IN 2080 |
|---|---|---|
| | Too Warm | Too Warm |
| | Cold Enough | Cold Enough |
| | Cold Enough | May Be Too Warm |
| | Too Warm | Too Warm |
| | May Be Too Warm | Too Warm |
| | Cold Enough | Cold Enough |
| | Too Warm | Too Warm |
| | May Be Too Warm | Too Warm |
| | Too Warm | Too Warm |
| | Cold Enough | Cold Enough |
| | May Be Too Warm | Too Warm |
| | Cold Enough | Cold Enough |
| | Cold Enough | Cold Enough |
| | Cold Enough | May Be Too Warm |
| | Cold Enough | Too Warm |
| | Cold Enough | Too Warm |
| | Cold Enough | Too Warm |
| | Too Warm | Too Warm |
| | Too Warm | Too Warm |
| | Cold Enough | Cold Enough |
| | Cold Enough | Cold Enough |

# Finding Hosts

Some cities are not able to host. Others do not want to. They look at past Games. There have been many problems. It is becoming harder to find hosts. This happened with the 2022 Winter Games. Several cities **withdrew** bids. Only two were left. Beijing was chosen to hold the event.

There was trouble with the 2024 Games too. Four cities backed out. Only two kept their bids. They were Los Angeles and Paris. The IOC felt it had to act. It picked two cities at the same time. This was a first. Paris would hold the 2024 Games. Los Angeles would host in 2028.

**FAST FACT:** Beijing hosted the Summer Games in 2008. It will host the Winter Games in 2022. It is the first city to host both events.

# Helping Out

The IOC wants to help. It is making changes to its rules. One now allows hosts to use existing buildings. This is good for cities like Tokyo. The 1964 Games were held there. Many structures remain. They can be used again in 2020. A stadium is still needed though. That alone will cost billions.

## ADDING A SPORT

Olympic sports and events are always changing. Nearly 100 events have been added since 1980. It is a long process. A sport must first apply to the IOC. There are many rules. One is that a sport cannot depend on motors. This has kept out car racing. A sport cannot use the mind alone either. This rules out chess. It must also be a sport that the public likes.

Six sports have been added for the 2020 Games. Baseball and softball are returning. They haven't been played since 2008. Four new sports are also being added. They are rock climbing, karate, surfing, and skateboarding.

# Fixed Sites

Some say more change is needed. They have an idea. The Games should have **fixed** sites. These would be called Olympic Parks. They would be owned by the IOC.

Can the IOC afford this? Many say yes. It gets money from **broadcast** rights. Companies could also be sponsors. Countries would help out too.

There is one big question. Where should the sites be? Athens is one option. Greece is where the first contests were held. It is a fitting location for the Summer Games.

Athletes have a place to shine. Countries show their pride. People from around the world tune in. These are the Olympics. The future of the event is uncertain. But one thing is clear. The Games bring us all closer together.

**FAST FACT:** The first Olympic torch relay was at the 1936 Games. Over 3,000 runners took part. The relay began in Olympia. It ended in Berlin. The route took 12 days to finish.

# Glossary

**bankrupt:** unable to pay back money that is owed

**benefit:** a good outcome

**bid:** to make an offer on something you want

**boycott:** to refuse to take part in an event as a way of protesting

**broadcast:** sharing on radio or TV

**conflict:** differences that keep groups from agreeing

**cyberattack:** an attempt to access a computer system with the intent to cause damage or harm

**debt:** money that is owed

**drug test:** a test that shows if someone has used illegal or banned substances

**fixed:** in a place that does not change

**hacker:** a person who breaks into computer databases

**intense:** extreme; very challenging

**responsible:** in charge of making sure that an event happens smoothly

**retire:** to stop working at a job or career

**revival:** when something becomes popular again after a long time

**sponsor:** a person or organization that pays for something in exchange for advertising

**tax:** money paid to a government for services

**underdog:** a person or team that is expected to lose

**unite:** to bring together

**withdraw:** to take something back

# TAKE A LOOK INSIDE
# WORLD CUP
# SOCCER

# CHAPTER 3

## How the World Cup Works

The idea behind the World Cup is simple. Every country can enter a team. These teams compete in tournaments. One team wins. It is the world champion of soccer.

The final tournament lasts about a month. But the process begins long before that. Qualification is the first stage. This lasts two years. There are only 32 spots available. Hundreds of countries want one. They compete to qualify. Games happen around the world. Nearby teams play each other. Top ones go to the final tournament.

### WHERE PLAYERS COME FROM

Most players at the World Cup are professionals. They get paid to play on other teams. These teams are called clubs. Famous clubs include Manchester United in England, Real Madrid in Spain, Juventus in Italy, Corinthians in Brazil, and Boca Juniors in Argentina. Clubs play each other in regional leagues. The U.S. and Canada share a professional soccer league called Major League Soccer (MLS). It includes teams such as the LA Galaxy, Seattle Sounders, Toronto FC, and New York Red Bulls.

### FIFA Confederations

FIFA divides the world into six regions. They call these confederations. Each holds qualifying tournaments. The top teams in each region go to the World Cup.

| REGION | CONFEDERATION NAME |
|---|---|
| Africa | Confédération Africaine de Football (CAF) |
| Asia and Australia | Asian Football Confederation (AFC) |
| Europe | Union des Associations Européennes de Football (UEFA) |
| North and Central America | The Confederation of North, Central America and Caribbean Association Football (CONCACAF) |
| Oceania | Oceania Football Confederation (OFC) |
| South America | Confederación Sudamericana de Fútbol (CONMEBOL) |

# CHAPTER 6

# Shock and Scandal

Thousands of people work together to put on each World Cup. Billions of dollars are spent. Usually, everything goes smoothly. But occasionally there are twists.

## Red Card Drama

Stress runs high at games. Players sometimes lose their cool. They might break the rules. Some argue or fight. When this happens, the referee can take action. He shows a red card. The player has to leave the field. No one can replace him for the rest of the game. His team is left short a player. It is a difficult position to be in. Red cards can change World Cup matches.

David Beckham was a young star. In 1998, he went to his first World Cup. He played for England. His team went up against Argentina. It was a knockout round. The score was tied. All eyes were on Beckham.

Then the star lost his temper. He kicked a player. This got him a red card. Beckham was sent off the field. England lost. Many called it a disaster. Some fans never forgave him.

### DRACULA ON THE FIELD

It was the 2014 World Cup. Luis Suárez was playing for Uruguay. He clashed with an opponent. Then he did something unusual. Suárez sank his teeth into the player's shoulder. Fans gasped. The player showed his bite marks. But the referee did not give a red card. Many people were outraged. It was the third time Suárez had bit someone during a match. There was an odd twist. This ref had a nickname. It was Dracula. Some thought he looked like an actor who played the vampire on TV. Fans started calling Suárez "Dracula" too. FIFA suspended him for nine games. He was also banned from all soccer activities for four months.

## American Stars

Many players on the U.S. women's team became superstars. They inspired a new generation. More kids wanted to play soccer.

Michelle Akers was there from the start. She played in the team's first-ever game. This was in 1985. In 1991, she scored ten goals at the first Women's World Cup. She led the team to victory again in 1999. Akers got an award in 2000. FIFA named her Women's Player of the Century.

Mia Hamm

Carli Lloyd

Mia Hamm is one of the country's most famous players. She had two World Cup wins. Her career also included two Olympic gold medals. Hamm won the FIFA award for best women's player twice. In 2007, she got into the National Soccer Hall of Fame.

Carli Lloyd was a star in the 2015 Women's World Cup. She was the first woman player to score three goals during a final. It only took her 16 minutes to do it. FIFA named her the best women's player in 2015. Lloyd won in 2016 too.

Michelle Akers

# WH☇TE L☇GHTNING BOOKS®

## NONFICTION

**CRYPTOCURRENCY**
BY M.G. HIGGINS

9781680216387

**DEADLY BITES**
BY M.G. HIGGINS

9781680216400

**DIGITAL WORLDS**
BY EMILY SCHLESINGER

9781680217377

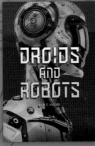

**DROIDS AND ROBOTS**
BY M.G. HIGGINS

9781680216394

**ESPORTS**
BY M.G. HIGGINS

9781680217391

**FLIGHT SQUADS**
BY EMILY SCHLESINGER

9781680216912

**OLYMPIC GAMES**
BY M.G. HIGGINS

9781680217384

**WORKING DOGS**
BY M.G. HIGGINS

9781680217414

**WORLD CUP SOCCER**
BY EMILY SCHLESINGER

9781680217407

## MORE TITLES COMING SOON
SDLBACK.COM/WHITE-LIGHTNING-BOOKS